SH*T GIRLS SAY

SH*T
GIRLS
SAY

KYLE HUMPHREY and GRAYDON SHEPPARD

First published in Great Britain by
Fourth Estate
a division of HarperCollinsPublishers
77–85 Fulham Palace Road
London W6 8JB
www.4thestate.co.uk
First published in the US and Canada by Harlequin 2012

1 3 5 7 9 10 8 6 4 2

A catalogue record for this book is available from the British Library

ISBN 978-0-00-749780-5

Printed in Spain by Graficas Estella

We dedicate this book to our mothers, sisters, grandmothers, aunts, and nieces.

FRIENDS
&
FASHION

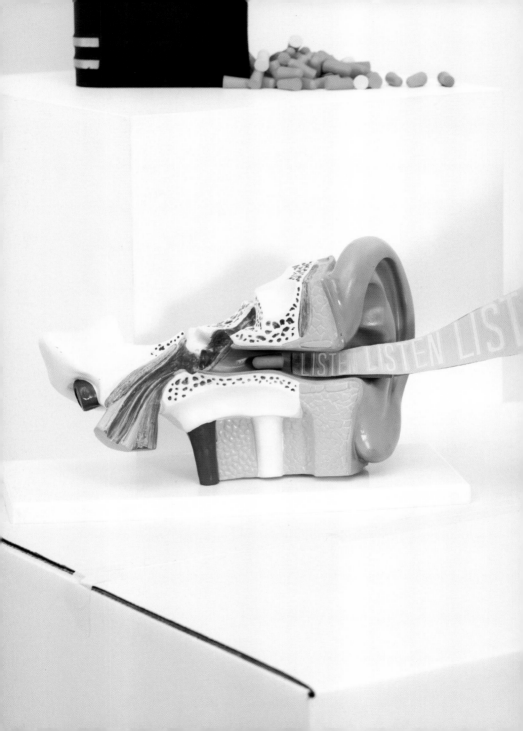

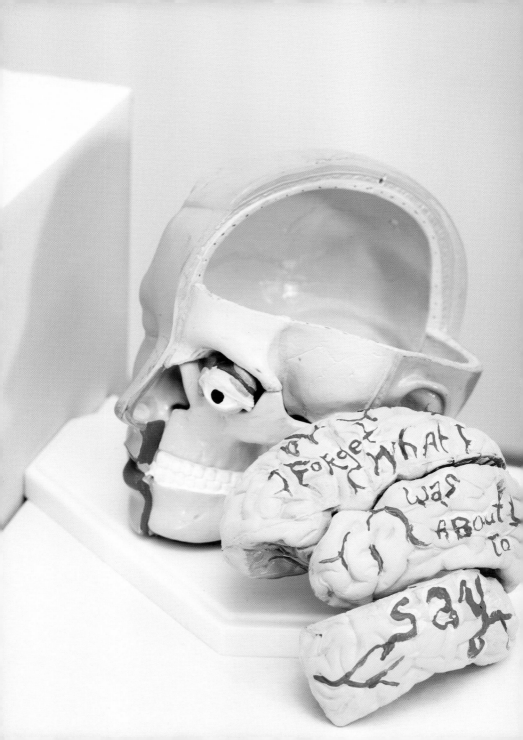

I'm so sick of all my clothes.

FROM STRANGER TO EX

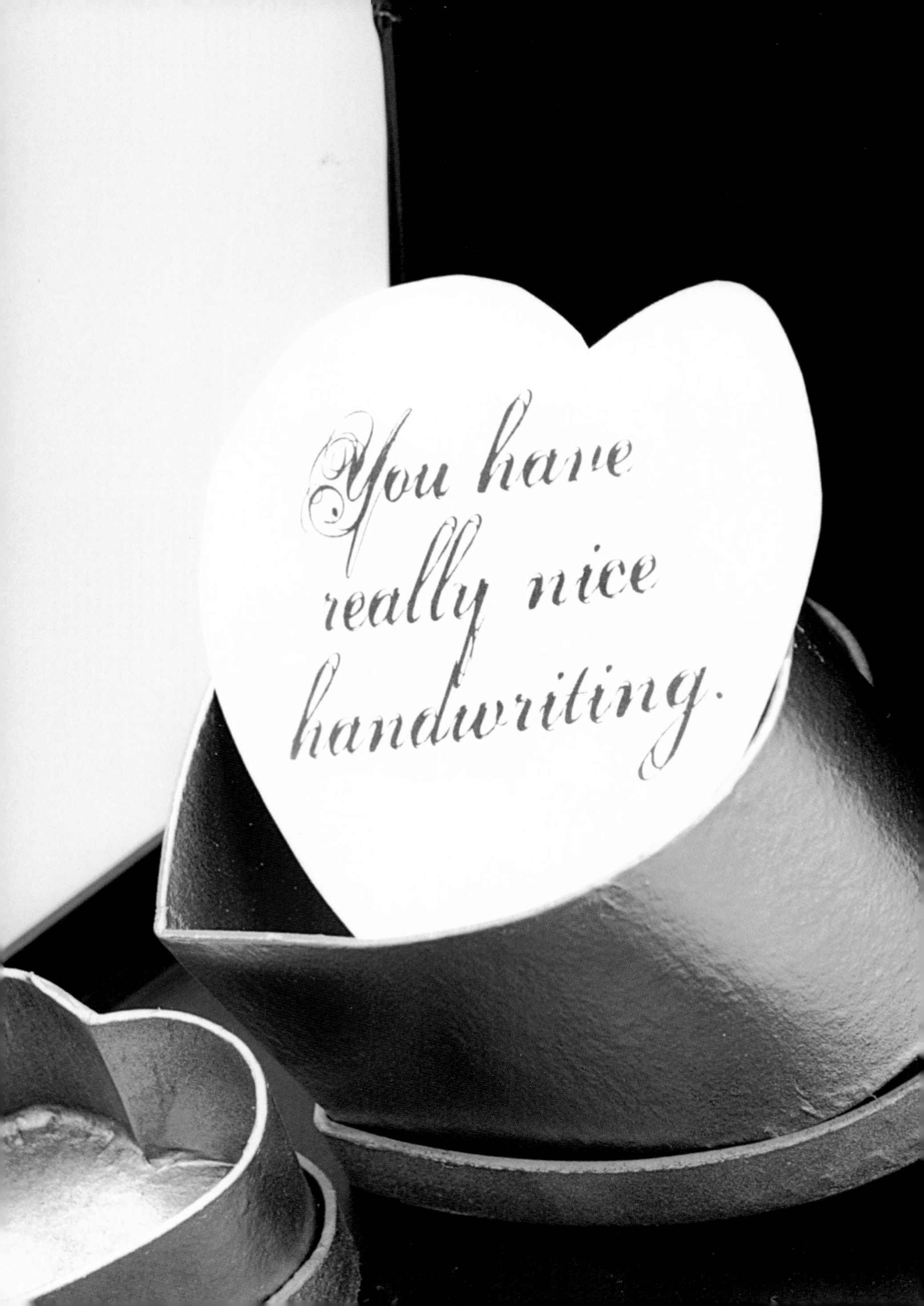
You have
really nice
handwriting.

I have the

BEST boyfriend.

Hey, where are you?

Did you miss me?

I'm excited for our date this week!

Was I super annoying last night?

My phone's being stupid.

Your phone must be off.

Are we in a fight?

BODY

ISSUES

I think I need braces.

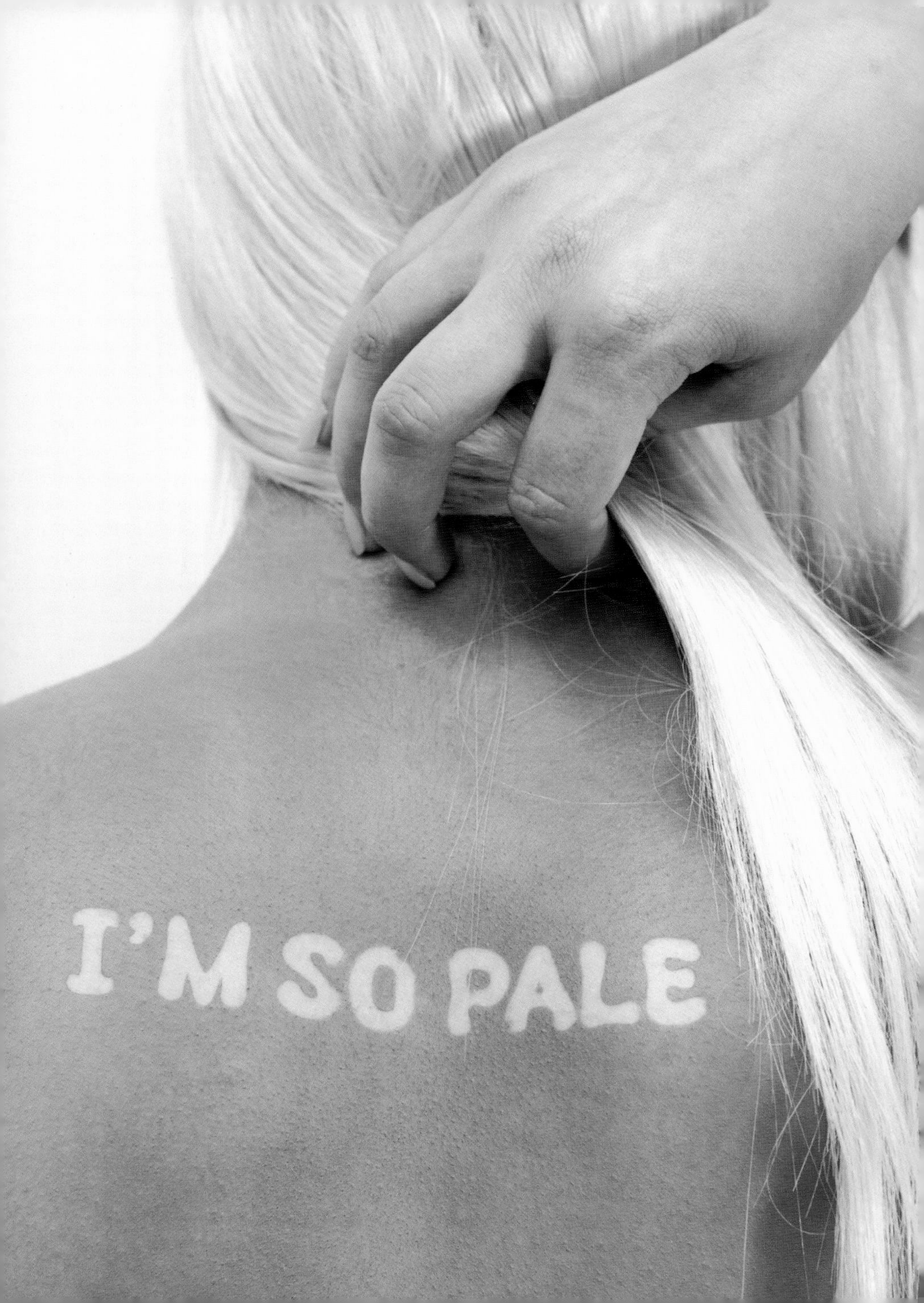
I'M SO PALE

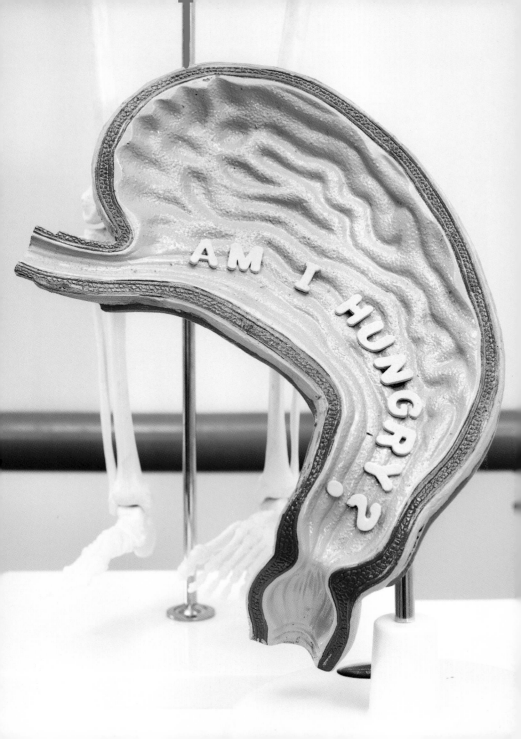

I CAN'T BELIEVE I ATE

ALL THAT

GETTING SICK.

COULD
YOU PASS
ME THAT
BLANKET?

COULD
YOU PASS
ME THAT
BLANKET?

COULD
YOU PASS
ME THAT
BLANKET?

COULD
YOU PASS
ME THAT
BLANKET?

COULD
YOU PASS
ME THAT
BLANKET?

COULD
YOU PASS
ME THAT
BLANKET?

COULD
YOU PASS
ME THAT
BLANKET?

COULD
YOU PASS
ME THAT
BLANKET?

COULD
YOU PASS
ME THAT
BLANKET?

COULD
YOU PASS
ME THAT
BLANKET?

COULD
YOU PASS
ME THAT
BLANKET?

COULD
YOU PASS
ME THAT
BLANKET?

COULD
YOU PASS
ME THAT
BLANKET?

COULD
YOU PASS
ME THAT
BLANKET?

COULD
YOU PASS
ME THAT
BLANKET?

COULD
YOU PASS
ME THAT
BLANKET?

COULD
YOU PASS
ME THAT
BLANKET?

COULD
YOU PASS
ME THAT
BLANKET?

SMALL TALK AT THE PARTY

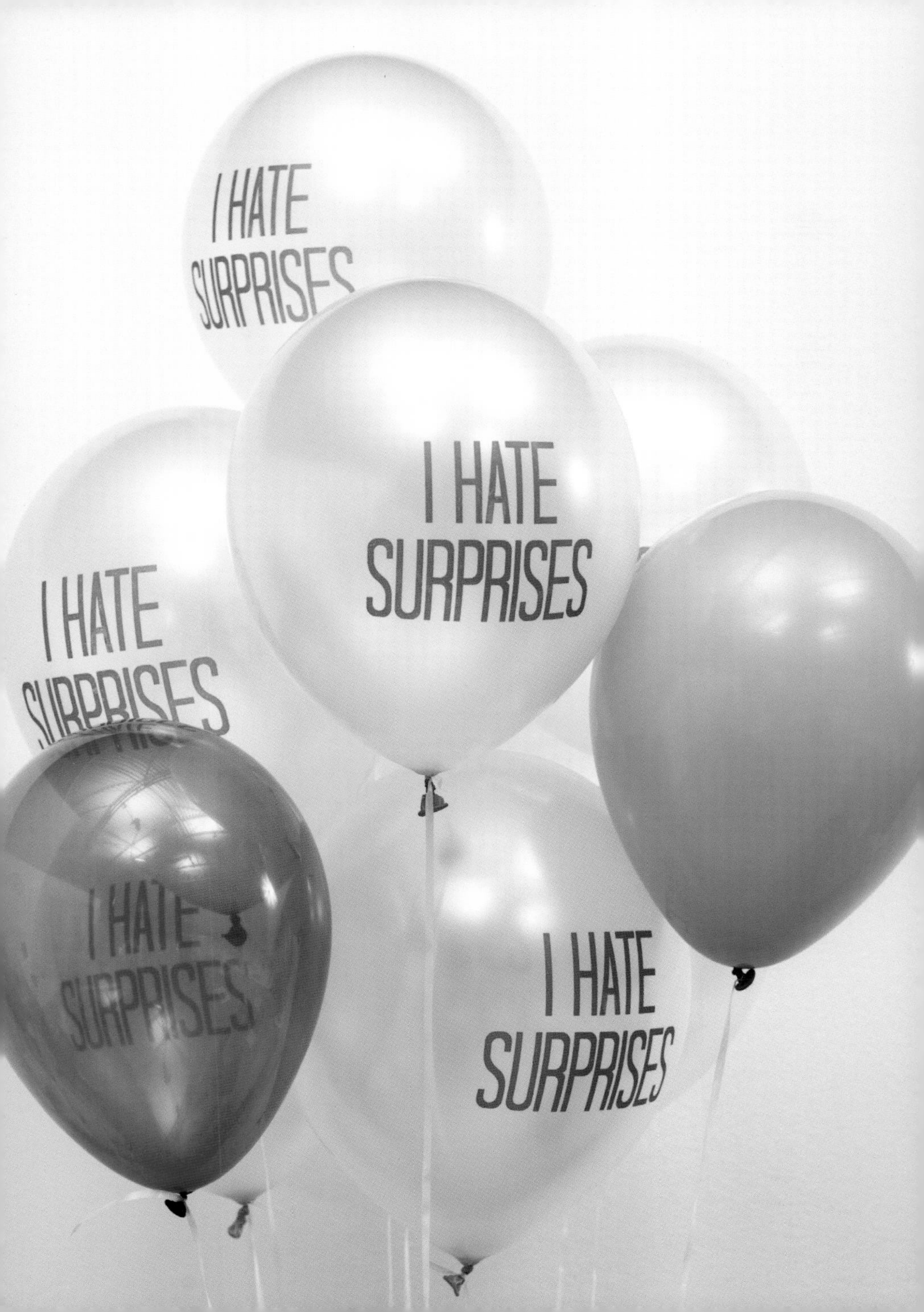

What if we did a bake sale?

you're such a good gift-given.

WHAT'S YOUR
DOG'S NAME?

I'll have
a glass of
prosecco.

EMOTIONS
&
INSECURITIES

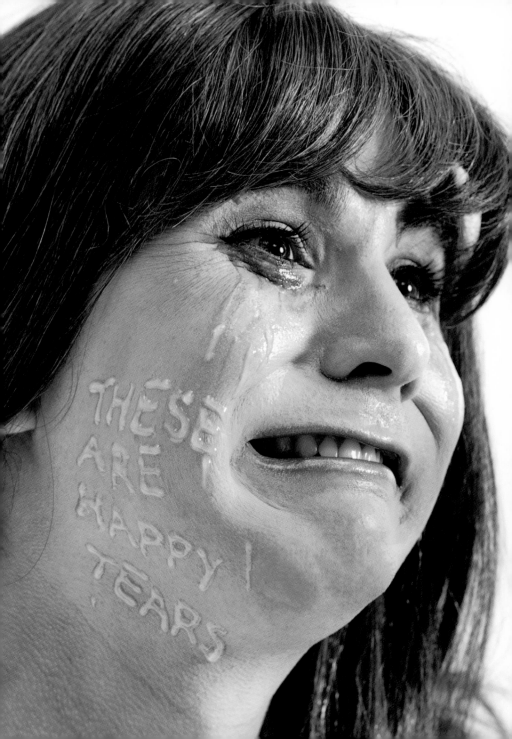

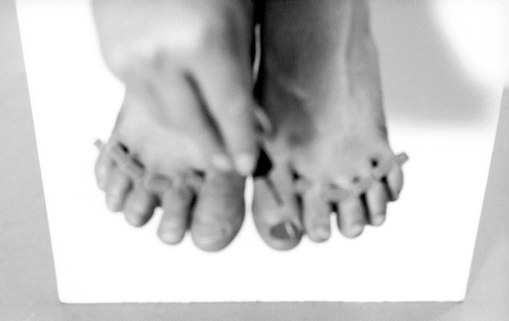

I wish I had
time to
meditate.

Life is about the journey

...not the destination.

Kyle would like to thank:

Madison, Mom, Dad, Gummy, Gumpy,
Grandma Marge and Grandpa Helge

Graydon would like to thank:

Gramma, Mom, Dad, John, Andrew and Cindy,
Kristen and Robert, Laura and Scott,
Maeve, Lila, Will and Cole

We would like to thank:

Deb Brody,
Simon Green, Emma Thaler, and the CAA team,
Shara Alexander, Jessica Rosenberg, Maria Ribas,
Sandra Valentine, Natasa Hatsios, Gigi Lau, Margie Miller,
Amy Jones, Debbie Soares, Nicki Kommit, Larissa Walker,
Arina Kharlamova, Reka Rubin, Christine Tsai,
Donna Hayes, Loriana Sacilotto, Craig Swinwood,
Brent Lewis, Alex Osuszek, and the Harlequin team,
Michael Lasker, Brent Lilley, Justin Letter,
Ryan Pastorek, Gregg Gellman,
Kirsten Nichols, Pamela Hamilton,
Sioban Quigley, Beaux Lewis-Quigley,
Margot Arakelian, Charlotte Glynn,
Christian Buer, David Chang, Ann Cockfield,
Juliette Lewis, Stacy London, Abby Elliott,
Ali Adler, Michael Ian Black, Jiffy Wild

About the Authors

Kyle Humphrey is a graphic designer, visual artist, and writer.

Graydon Sheppard is a writer, director, and the star of *Shit Girls Say*.

Kyle and Graydon are the co-creators of *Shit Girls Say*, which started as a Twitter account in 2011 and evolved into a viral YouTube sensation later that year. The videos have garnered over 30 million views.

www.kyledavidlarsenhumphrey.com
www.graydonsheppard.com

www.ShitGirlsSay.com